Introduction & C

A short while ago, we published Tina Cox's first Patter her clever and innovative Straight Border Pattern Gri

The little ii-Book has been a resounding success, and parchers across the globe have embraced her smart and simple approach to what is often considered an arduous, advanced process: GRIDWORK

Once you get into Parchment Craft, you soon want to master that fabulous lacework which parchers so often use to frame their artwork. Traditionally, it is quite complicated and requires lots of counting and focus! Tina has developed a brilliant series of Border Pattern Grids, both straight and diagonal, to help you create beautiful gridwork and lacework easily.

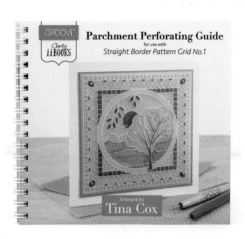

In case you missed the first STRAIGHT PATTERN BORDER, and are starting out here with the DIAGONAL PATTERN BORDER No. 1, it matters not. The concept is the same, the technique is the same. The only difference is that the holes in the grid are offset (diagonal), so the patterns are completely new.

Tools you'll need

Clarity Lightwave
A4 Translucent Piercing Mat
Groovi Plate Starter Kit
Groovi Border Plate Mate
Groovi Baby Plate Mate
Border Pattern Grid Diagonal No. 1
Diagonal Basic Piercing Grid
Groovi Single Needle Perforating Tool or
Pergamano Bold 1-needle tool
Pergamano 1mm ball tool
Pergamano 3mm ball tool
Pergamano 4.5mm ball tool
Pergamano Mapping Pen
Pergamano Sticky Ink
Ultra Fine Perga Glitter
Pergamano Dorso Oil
Groovi Guard
Groovi Sticker Tabs

The Grid

This Border Pattern Grid comprises seven basic patterns.

These pattern grids can be used to emboss or perforate.

Emboss from the back and perforate from the front.

Perforated & Embossed

Here we see each of the seven patterns either embossed or perforated along a straight line, just as they come on the pattern grid.

You can also combine embossing and perforating to produce beautiful lacework. See instructions below and overleaf.

Perforating & Embossing

COMBINED

1. If starting with embossing

a. Attach parchment on pattern grid, back facing up.
b. Emboss pattern with No. 2 ball tool from Groovi Starter Kit, or 1mm Pergamano ball tool.
c. Remove from grid.
d. Turn parchment around, line up embossed dots on diagonal basic grid & attach.
e. Perforate design between embossed dots using 1-needle bold tool.

2. If starting with perforating

a. Attach parchment on pattern grid, front facing up.
b. Perforate pattern with 1-needle bold tool.
c. Remove from grid.
d. Turn parchment over, line up perforated holes on diagonal basic grid and attach.
e. Emboss the design between the perforated holes, again using the No. 2 or the 1mm ball tool.

6

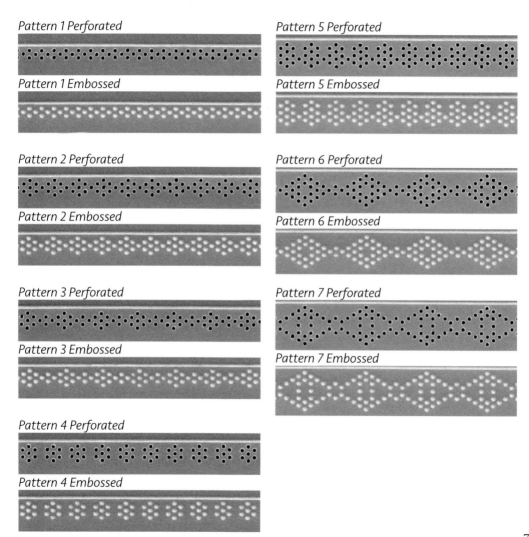

Pattern 1 Perforated

Pattern 1 Embossed

Pattern 2 Perforated

Pattern 2 Embossed

Pattern 3 Perforated

Pattern 3 Embossed

Pattern 4 Perforated

Pattern 4 Embossed

Pattern 5 Perforated

Pattern 5 Embossed

Pattern 6 Perforated

Pattern 6 Embossed

Pattern 7 Perforated

Pattern 7 Embossed

7

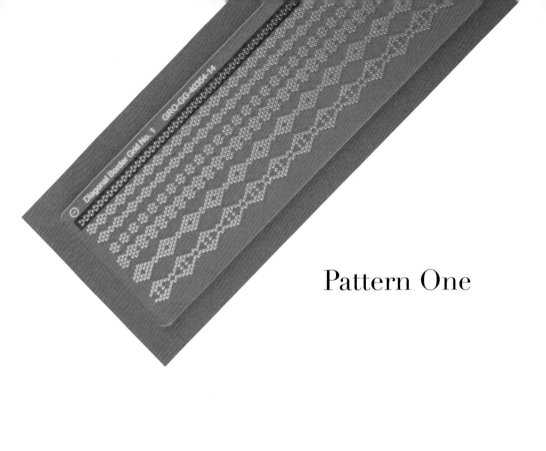

Pattern One

Pattern One, Perforated & Embossed

A QUICK HOW-TO USING PATTERN ONE

The following is a guide to perforating and embossing the first pattern on the grid along a straight line. The images and instructions explain how to combine embossing and perforating techniques in order to create various patterns that can be used in your parchment craft designs. Pages 10 to 15 contain examples of completed card projects, designed by Tina Cox. Each card presents an example of how this first pattern can be used to embellish your parchment art. These quick how-to guides, and example projects are repeated throughout the book for each of the seven patterns on the grid.

Example 1

1. Emboss top and bottom of pattern 1 only.

2. Turn to front & perforate the middle row.

Example 2

1. Using pattern 1, emboss one row.

2. Turn to front & perforate on diagonal grid.

Example 3

1. Using pattern 1, perforate a zig-zag.

2. Turn to back & emboss dots on the inside, using a diagonal grid.

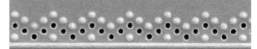

3. Then emboss a zig-zag on the outside.

Lady's Day at the Races

DESIGNED USING PATTERN ONE

Ingredients

Groovi Grids: *Diagonal Border Pattern Grid No.1* GRO-GG-40354-14, *Diagonal Basic Piercing Grid Border* GRO-GG-40383-14.
Groovi Baby Plates: *Art Deco Lady* GRO-PE-40178-01.
Groovi Border Plates: *Funky Henna* GRO-PA-40157-09.
Groovi A5² Plates: *Nested Squares* GRO-PA-40037-03.

To Make

1. Emboss the centrepiece and swirly flourish design on regular parchment paper first. Then continue with the double square frame; this way the flourish can sit on top because you embossed it first.

2. Colour on the back. vibrant Perga Colours will work well with these tiny areas.

3. Emboss dots on top of the hat and inside the flowerburst.

4. Perforate dots for the inside of the hat.

5. Emboss and perforate Border Pattern 1 in the double outlined square (see example 1 on page 9).

6. Emboss Border Pattern 1 outside the square.

7. Cut and mount on pink parchment, then black card using brads, then lastly onto a white card blank.

Mosaic Blue

DESIGNED USING PATTERN ONE

Ingredients

Groovi Grids: *Diagonal Border Pattern Grid No.1* GRO-GG-40354-14,
Diagonal Basic Piercing Grid Border GRO-GG-40383-14.
Groovi A5² Plates: *Nested Squares* GRO-PA-40037-03,
Nested Circles GRO-PA-40051-03, *Nested Octagon* GRO-PA-40119-03,
Snowflakes GRO-CH-40018-03, *Large Lace Netting* GRO-PA-40339-03.

To Make

1. Emboss design on blue parchment paper. It is best to start with the central image - in this case the snowflake - and work your way outwards.

2. Colour on back. Perga Colour pens are ideal for this kind of mosaic look.

3. Emboss and perforate Border Pattern 1 between both double outlined squares.

4. Emboss and perforate Border Pattern 1 around the outside edge, too (see example 2 on page 9).

5. Emboss Border Pattern 1 between the circle and octagon.

6. Cut and mount on blue parchment, then black card using brads. Finally, mount on a white card blank.

Meadow Grasses

DESIGNED USING PATTERN ONE

Ingredients

Groovi Grids: *Diagonal Border Pattern Grid No.1* GRO-GG-40354-14,
Diagonal Basic Piercing Grid Border GRO-GG-40383-14.
Groovi A5² Plates: *Nested Squares* GRO-PA-40037-03,
Meadow Grasses GRO-GR-40006-03, *Flourish Frame* GRO-FL-40219-03.

To Make

1. Emboss design on pink parchment paper, starting with the flourish. This will help you decide which squares to emboss on the outside and the inner area.

2. Colour on back. Blend Perga Liners with Dorso oil for a rich, soft effect.

3. Emboss and perforate Border Pattern 1 outside both square outlines (see example 3 on page 9).

4. Cut and mount on another layer of regular parchment (this will lighten the overall colour), then dark pink parchment, then black card using brads, then onto a white card blank.

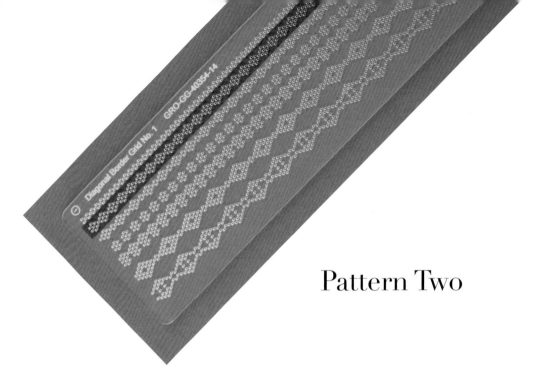

Pattern Two

Pattern Two, Perforated & Embossed

A QUICK HOW-TO USING PATTERN TWO

Example 1

1. Emboss pattern from the back.

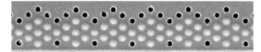

2. Turn to the front and perforate a zig-zag on top and a single dot between the shapes using a diagonal grid.

Example 2

1. Perforate as shown from the front.

2. Turn to the back & emboss dots on the inside, then a zig-zag on the outside, using a diagonal grid.

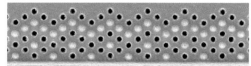

3. Turn to the front again, and perforate a zig-zag.

Example 3

1. Perforate as shown from the front.

2. Turn to the back & emboss dots between.

3. Then top and bottom using diagonal grid.

3. Turn over and perforate on diagonal grid.

Jayne's Dahlias

DESIGNED USING PATTERN TWO

Ingredients

Groovi Grids: *Diagonal Border Pattern Grid No.1* GRO-GG-40354-14,
Diagonal Basic Piercing Grid Border GRO-GG-40383-14.
Groovi Border Plates: *Lace 1* GRO-PA-40044-09.
Groovi A5² Plates: *Nested Squares* GRO-PA-40037-03,
Jayne's Dahlias GRO-FL-40389-03.

To Make

1. Emboss design on regular parchment paper. Be sure to leave a gap at the base of the dahlia large enough to take the pattern.

2. Once you have wrapped the lace design around the double-outlined square, add some light whitework on the outer lace area and the tips of the dahlia petals.

3. Colour in on the back, using Perga Liners and Perga Colours.

4. Emboss Border Pattern 2 inside the double outlined square (see example 1 on page 17).

5. Emboss and perforate Border Pattern 2 inside the inner square.

6. Cut and mount on blue parchment and black card with brads. Wrap a length of organza ribbon around the piece and mount it on a white card blank. Now tie a bow in the centre to finish.

Happy Christmas

DESIGNED USING PATTERN TWO

Ingredients

Groovi Grids: *Diagonal Border Pattern Grid No.1* GRO-GG-40354-14, *Diagonal Basic Piercing Grid Border* GRO-GG-40383-14.
Groovi Border Plates: *Just To Say Line Sentiment* GRO-WO-40103-09.
Groovi A5² Plates: *Nested Squares* GRO-PA-40037-03.
Groovi A4² Plates: *Jayne Nestorenko Winter Scenes* GRO-WI-40501-15.

To Make

1. Emboss the design on pink parchment paper. There's a sequence here. Start with the square frame and apertures first, leaving enough space for the Line Sentiment. Do all the gridwork next. The last thing to add is the Winter Scene. That way, you can emboss the scene right up to the gridwork.

2. Emboss Border Pattern 2 inside the lower rectangle.

3. Emboss and perforate Border Pattern 2 in the upper rectangle and outside the main square (see example 2 on page 17).

4. Now introduce the Winter Scene. Do some gentle whitework on the hills and snowman, and colour carefully on the back with either pencils or pens.

5. Cut and mount on regular parchment, then attach to black card with brads. Mount this on a white card blank.

6. Add sparkle using a Mapping Pen, Sticky Ink and ultra fine Perga-Glitter.

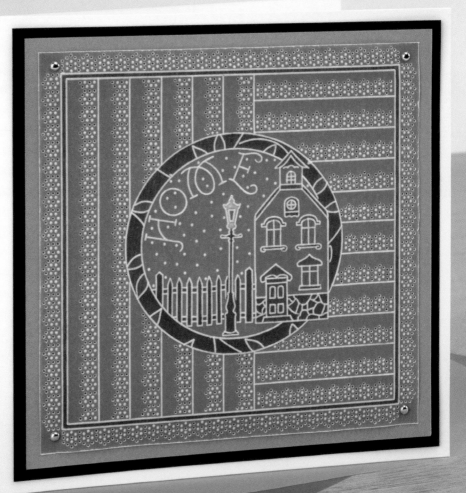

Home

Ingredients

Groovi Grids: *Diagonal Border Pattern Grid No.1* GRO-GG-40354-14,
Diagonal Basic Piercing Grid Border GRO-GG-40383-14.
Groovi Baby Plates: *Wee Houses & Shops* GRO-HO-40344-01
Groovi A5² Plates: *Nested Squares* GRO-PA-40037-03,
Nested Circles GRO-PA-40051-03.
Groovi A4² Plates: *Alphabet Picture Frame* GRO-FL-40397-15.

To Make

1. Emboss on blue parchment paper. Whatever sits at the front of the composition must be embossed first. In this case, it's the house. So start with the house and then move to the circular double-frame. The rest of the design either sits inside or outside that frame.

2. Add the lettering and snow inside the circle.

3. Colour on the back, using dark Perga Colour pens.

4. Use the Nested Square to establish tramlines, then emboss and perforate Border Pattern 2 along the lines inside, and then outside the whole square frame (see example 3 on page 17).

5. Cut and mount on regular parchment and black card using brads. Attach to a white card blank to finish.

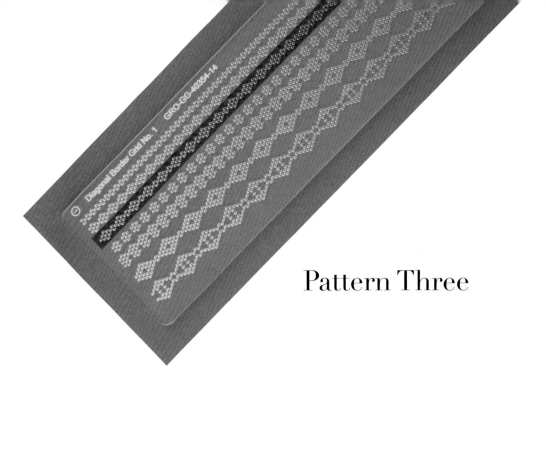

Pattern Three

Pattern Three, Perforated & Embossed

A QUICK HOW-TO USING PATTERN THREE

Example 1

1. Emboss partial pattern.

2. Turn to the front and perforate the rest.

Example 2

1. Perforate as shown.

2. Turn to the back & emboss dots using a diagonal grid.

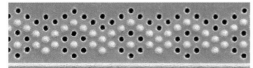

3. Turn to the front again, and perforate on the diagonal grid.

Example 3

1. Emboss entire pattern.

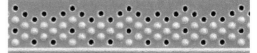

2. Perforate as shown, using a diagonal grid.

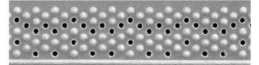

3. Turn over and emboss a 'fill' of dots at the top, above the perforated zig-zag.

The Bashful Owl

Ingredients

Groovi Grids: *Diagonal Border Pattern Grid No.1* GRO-GG-40354-14, *Diagonal Basic Piercing Grid Border* GRO-GG-40383-14.
Groovi Baby Plates: *Wren & Leaves* GRO-BI-40212-01, *Branches* GRO-TR-40346-01, *Owl Plate* NEW DESIGN GROOVI® CLUB BACK ISSUE 11.
Groovi A5² Plates: *Nested Squares* GRO-PA-40037-03, *Nested Octagons* GRO-PA-40119-03, *Textures Plate* GRO-PA-40224-03.

To Make

1. Emboss the owl and lower branch on regular parchment. Wrap the double octagon shape around it, and then add the square double frame. Once these are in place, you can go back and add the other upper branch and the chequer corners.

2. Colour in the owl, chequer corners and leaves from the back, using Perga Liners and Dorso oil to blend. For very tight lines like the branches, a Perga Colour pen is perfect.

3. Emboss and perforate random 'daisies' on and around the branch using Border Pattern 4.

4. Emboss and perforate Border Pattern 3 inside the double outlined octagon (see example 1 on page 25).

5. Cut and mount on pink parchment and black card using brads, then attach to a white card blank.

Have a Great Day

Ingredients

Groovi Grids: *Diagonal Border Pattern Grid No.1* GRO-GG-40354-14,
Diagonal Basic Piercing Grid Border GRO-GG-40383-14.
Groovi Border Plates: *Cake Decorations* GRO-WE-40377-09,
Nested Tags GRO-PA-40122-09.
Groovi A5² Plates: *Nested Squares* GRO-PA-40037-03, *Happy Birthday*
GRO-WO-40276-03, *Sprig Background* GRO-FL-40008-03, *Ribbons & Bows*
GRO-LW-40435-03, *Textures Plate* GRO-PA-40224-03.

To Make

1. Emboss the design on blue parchment, starting with the ribbon bow at the front, then the tag, then the outer square frame. The wonderful sprig background can be added after that.

2. Colour on the back using Perga Colour pens or Distress Markers.

3. Emboss and perforate with Border Pattern 3 outside the square, and cut to size.

4. Emboss and perforate with Border Pattern 3 on regular parchment paper. Create two strips that are longer than the diagonals so they can be tucked behind the backing card (see example 2 on page 25).

6. Mount the blue parchment on regular parchment and black card, using brads.

7. Attach the ribbon strips so that they are tucked behind the black card and then attach to a white card blank.

Merry Christmas

DESIGNED USING PATTERN THREE

Ingredients

Groovi Grids: *Diagonal Border Pattern Grid No.1* GRO-GG-40354-14, *Diagonal Basic Piercing Grid Border* GRO-GG-40383-14.
Groovi A5² Plates: *Nested Squares* GRO-PA-40037-03, *Merry Christmas* GRO-WO-40275-03, *Woven* GRO-PA-40097-03, *Snowflakes* GRO-CH-40018-03, *Swing On a Star* GRO-AL-40462-03.

To Make

1. Emboss the base design on pink parchment. Start with the Merry Christmas, make a square frame, add stars in the corners and then infill the woven boxes.

2. Emboss Border Pattern 3 in the woven boxes.

3. Colour on the back using Perga Colour pens. Great for tight areas.

4. Emboss and perforate Border Pattern 3 outside the square and cut to size (see example 3 on page 25).

5. Emboss three snowflakes on regular parchment and emboss dots using the diagonal basic piercing grid border. Colour on the back and cut out.

6. Attach the snowflakes to the card (brads work well),and add a little bling with liquid pearl dots.

7. Mount the pink parchment on regular parchment and black card using brads. Attach to a white card blank.

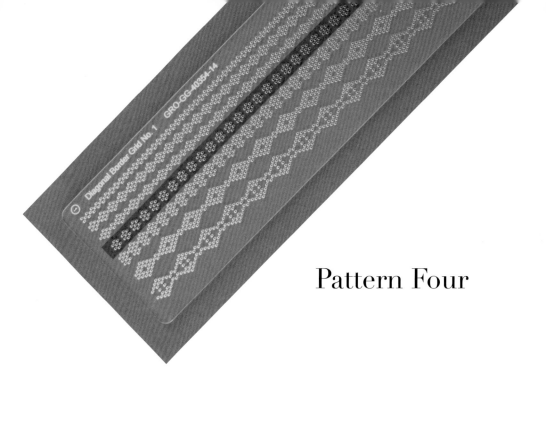

Pattern Four

Pattern Four, Perforated & Embossed

A QUICK HOW-TO USING PATTERN FOUR

Example 1

1. Emboss pattern.

2. Turn over and perforate.

Example 2

1. Perforate pattern as shown.

2. Turn to back and emboss.

3. Transfer to diagonal grid and emboss.

Example 3

1. Emboss pattern.

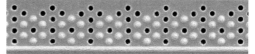

2. Turn over and perforate as shown on a diagonal grid.

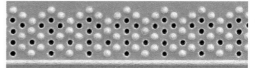

3. Turn to back and emboss on diagonal grid.

Celebrate Your special day

Celebrate Your Special Day

DESIGNED USING PATTERN FOUR

Ingredients

Groovi Grids: *Diagonal Border Pattern Grid No.1* GRO-GG-40354-14, *Diagonal Basic Piercing Grid Border* GRO-GG-40383-14.
Groovi A5² Plates: *Nested Squares* GRO-PA-40037-03, *Friends Are Like Flowers* GRO-GR-40443-03.
Groovi A4 Plates: *Wedding Cake Tem-plate* GRO-TE-40375-16.

To Make

1. Start with the double square frame and the central panel on regular parchment. Add the flower fields next, top and bottom, and finally emboss the words.

2. Colour on the back using either pencils with Dorso oil or pens - whichever you prefer.

3. Emboss and perforate Border Pattern 4 in the double outlined square (see example 1 on page 33).

4. Cut and mount on blue parchment layered on black card using brads. Attach to a white card blank.

5. On the front colour add a Wink of Stella for sparkle.

Eight little Daisies

DESIGNED USING PATTERN 4

Ingredients

Groovi Grids: *Diagonal Border Pattern Grid No.1* GRO-GG-40354-14,
Diagonal Basic Piercing Grid Border GRO-GG-40383-14.
Groovi Baby Plates: *Numbers Groovi Inset* GRO-WO-40133-11 *(use the oval shape).*
Groovi A5² Plates: *Nested Squares* GRO-PA-40037-03,
Ribbons & Bows GRO-LW-40435-03.
Groovi A4 Plates: *Wedding Cake Tem-Plate* GRO-TE-40375-16.

To Make

1. Emboss the design on dark pink parchment. Best to start with the double frame, 3rd/4th squares in. The rest will follow now.

2. Add a little gentle whitework to the daisies. Not only does it add whiteness, it also makes them stand proud. Colour on the back.

3. Emboss Border Pattern 4 inside the double outlined square and between the diamonds.

4. Emboss and perforate Border Pattern 4 outside the square and cut to size (see example 2 on page 33).

5. Emboss the bow on regular parchment and cut out.

6. Mount the bow and pink parchment on regular parchment. Mount on black card with brads. Attach the whole piece to a white card blank.

7. Add sparkle with a Wink of Stella.

Merry Christmas

Ingredients

Groovi Grids: *Diagonal Border Pattern Grid No.1* GRO-GG-40354-14,
Diagonal Basic Piercing Grid Border GRO-GG-40383-14.
Groovi A5² Plates: *Nested Squares* GRO-PA-40037-03.
Groovi A4 Plates: *Hearty Wreath* GRO-LW-40431-15,
Alphabet Picture Frame GRO-FL-40397-15, *Jayne's Winter Scene - Cat* STA-WI-40450-15.

To Make

1. Emboss your design on blue parchment, starting with the nested square, second square in.

2. Emboss dots in the corner decorations with Basic Diagonal Grid.

3. Colour in the tree on the back, using pens or pencils, whichever you prefer.

4. Emboss and perforate Border Pattern 4 in the rectangle panel (see example 3 on page 33). Be sure to leave a gap for the thin ribbon.

5. Cut and mount on regular parchment, and then on black card using brads.

6. Wrap the ribbon around the whole piece, and tie a dainty bow in between the lace border. Attach underneath the knot with Perga Glue.

7. Attach the whole piece to a white card blank.

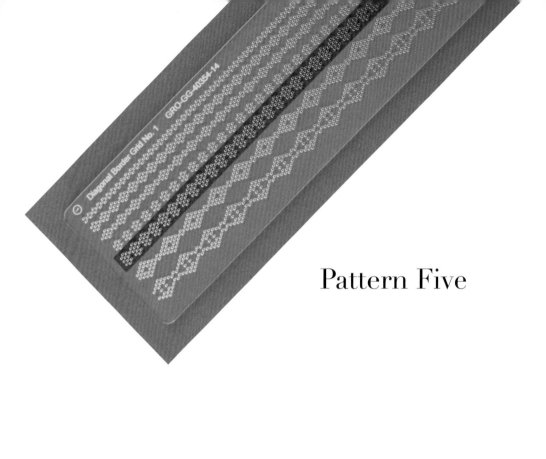

Pattern Five

Pattern Five, Perforated & Embossed

A QUICK HOW-TO USING PATTERN FIVE

Example 1

1. Emboss pattern.

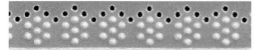

2. Turn to the front and perforate.

Example 2

1. Perforate pattern as shown.

2. Turn to back and emboss.

Example 3

1. Perforate pattern as shown.

2. Turn to back and emboss.

3. Turn and perforate a second line of hexagons.

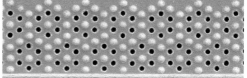

4. Transfer to diagonal grid, turn to the back and emboss.

The Hummingbird

DESIGNED USING PATTERN FIVE

Ingredients

Groovi Grids: *Diagonal Border Pattern Grid No.1* GRO-GG-40354-14, *Diagonal Basic Piercing Grid Border* GRO-GG-40383-14.

Groovi A5² Plates: *Nested Squares* GRO-PA-40037-03, *Christmas Doves* GRO-CH-40000-03, *Large Lace Netting* GRO-PA-40339-03, *Jayne's Hummingbirds* GRO-BI-40320-03.

Groovi A4² Plates: *Hearty Wreath* GRO-LW-40431-15.

To Make

1. Emboss your design on regular parchment, starting with the nested square, second square in. Look at the photo closely, to figure out which elements are added in which order...

2. Colour in on the back using Perga Colour pens and/or Distress Markers. Add a little soft whitework to the leaves in the wreath.

3. Emboss and perforate Border Pattern 5 in the corners and outside the square (see example 1 on page 41).

4. Cut and mount on pink parchment and black card using brads. Attach the entire piece to a white card blank.

5. Use a Wink of Stella pen to add sparkle on the front in the netting.

Dream, Laugh, Love.

DESIGNED USING PATTERN FIVE

Ingredients

Groovi Grids: *Diagonal Border Pattern Grid No.1* GRO-GG-40354-14, *Diagonal Basic Piercing Grid Border* GRO-GG-40383-14.
Groovi A5² Plates: *Nested Squares* GRO-PA-40037-03, *Universal Framer* GRO-CH-40306-01, *Textures* GRO-PA-40224-03, *Floral Circle* GRO-FL-40446-03, *Friends Are Like Flowers* GRO-GR-40443-03.

To Make

1. Emboss your design on blue parchment, starting with the Universal Framer. Then build boxes using the Nested Square. Just go for it! Fill them in as you like, but be sure to create contrast with neighbouring areas. Use the largest square in the Nested Squares to completely frame your work.

2. Colour on the back with Perga Colour pens. They are perfect for getting into small, tight areas.

3. Emboss and perforate Border Pattern 5 inside the large square frame (see example 2 on page 41).

4. Cut and mount on regular parchment and black card with brads. Attach your artwork to a white card blank.

Flower Power

Ingredients

Groovi Grids: *Diagonal Border Pattern Grid No.1* GRO-GG-40354-14, *Diagonal Basic Piercing Grid Border* GRO-GG-40383-14.

Groovi Baby Plates: *Vases* GRO-FL-40217-01.

Groovi Border Plates: *Funky Henna* GRO-PA-40157-09, *Henna Groovi Border* GRO-PA-40155-09.

Groovi A5² Plates: *Nested Squares* GRO-PA-40037-03, *Universal Framer* GRO-CH-40306-01.

To Make

1. Emboss your design on pink parchment. Build the boxes and panels, using the sixth nested square as the outer perimeter.

2. Colour in on the back, using Perga Colour pens and/or Distress Markers.

3. Emboss dots on the flower and pot using a diagonal grid.

4. Emboss Border Pattern 4 in double outlined square. The little flowers will fit perfectly (see example 1, page 31).

5. Emboss and perforate Border Pattern 5 outside the square, and a border-strip on regular parchment (see example 3, page 41).

6. Cut and mount the pink parchment on regular parchment and black card using brads. Tuck and fold the pattern strip around the black card before attaching.

7. Attach this whole piece to a white card blank.

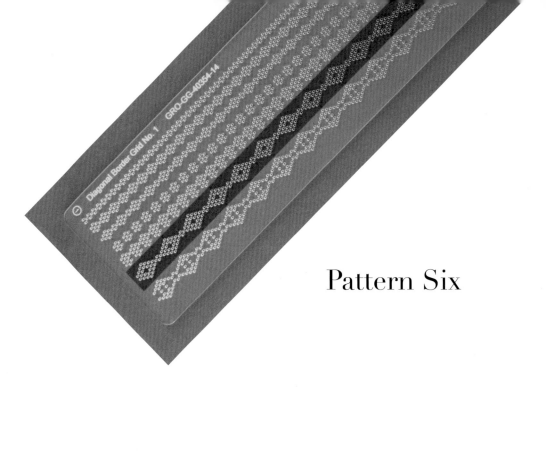

Pattern Six

Pattern Six, Perforated & Embossed

A QUICK HOW-TO USING PATTERN SIX

Example 1

1. Emboss pattern from the back.

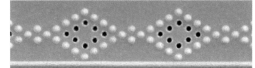

2. Turn to the front and perforate.

Example 2

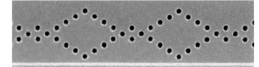

1. Perforate as shown.

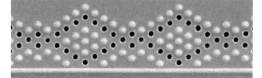

2. Turn to back and emboss on diagonal grid.

3. Turn to front and perforate on diagonal grid.

Example 3

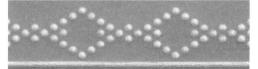

1. Emboss pattern.

2. Turn to front, perforate on diagonal grid.

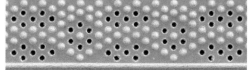

3. Turn to back and emboss on diagonal grid.

Special Day

Ingredients

Groovi Grids: *Diagonal Border Pattern Grid No.1* GRO-GG-40354-14, *Diagonal Basic Piercing Grid Border* GRO-GG-40383-14.
Groovi Baby Plates: *Vases* GRO-FL-40217-01.
Groovi Border Plates: *Cake Decoration* GRO-WE-40377-09.
Groovi A5² Plates: *Nested Squares* GRO-PA-40037-03, *Happy Birthday* GRO-WO-40276-03, *Textures* GRO-PA-40224-03, *Angels and Stars* GRO-AL-40463-03.

To Make

1. Emboss your design on regular parchment then use the nested square (second square in) to frame your work.

2. Colour in on the back, using Perga Colour pens.

3. Emboss and perforate Border Pattern 6 on the either side of the greetings panel (see example 1, page 49). Before you perforate, colour inside the diamonds.

4. Cut and mount on blue parchment and black card with brads. Attach to a white card blank.

5. Use a Wink of Stella pen to add sparkle.

Pink Bamboo

DESIGNED USING PATTERN SIX

Ingredients

Groovi Grids: *Diagonal Border Pattern Grid No.1* GRO-GG-40354-14, *Diagonal Basic Piercing Grid Border* GRO-GG-40383-14.
Groovi Border Plates: *Half Tone* GRO-PA-40156-09.
Groovi A5² Plates: *Nested Squares* GRO-PA-40037-03, *Bamboo* GRO-GR-40310-03, *Large Lace Netting* GRO-PA-40339-03.

To Make

1. Emboss your design on pink parchment. The outer nested square frame is using the third and fourth lines in. Leave the Half Tones circles until after you have added the gridwork. The Large Lace Netting creates a lovely pattern inside the double frame.

2. Apply some gentle whitework on the leaves and the bamboo on the back. Colour in on the back using Perga Liners for a soft look.

3. Emboss and perforate Border Pattern 6 on the right side of the sectioned square and outside the square (see example 2, page 49).

4. Cut and mount on regular parchment and black card with brads. Attach to a white card blank.

5. Use a Wink of Stella pen to add sparkle.

'Friends are Flowers
in the Garden of Life'

Friends are Flowers

DESIGNED USING PATTERN SIX

Ingredients

Groovi Grids: *Diagonal Border Pattern Grid No.1* GRO-GG-40354-14, *Diagonal Basic Piercing Grid Border* GRO-GG-40383-14.
Groovi Border Plates: *Lace 1 Border* GRO-PA-40044-09.
Groovi A5² Plates: *Nested Squares* GRO-PA-40037-03, *Friends are Flowers* GRO-GR-40443-03, *Floral Circle* GRO-FL-40446-03, *Angels and Stars* GRO-AL-40463-03. GRO-PA-40044-09

To Make

1. Emboss your design on blue parchment. Start with the outer frame (using the first and second squares in) and the panel for the words.

2. Fill in the Angels' dresses using the diagonal grid.

3. Colour in on the back using Perga Colour pens. Excellent for getting into tight areas.

4. Emboss and perforate Border Pattern 6 underneath the verse box and outside the square frame (see example 3, page 49).

5. Cut and mount on regular parchment and black card with brads. Attach to a white card blank.

6. Colour the flower centres with a Wink of Stella pen on the front.

Pattern Seven

Pattern Seven, Perforated & Embossed

A QUICK HOW-TO USING PATTERN SEVEN

Example 1

1. Emboss pattern.

2. Turn to front and perforate.

3. Turn to back and emboss on diagonal grid.

Example 2

1. Emboss pattern.

2. Turn to front and perforate.

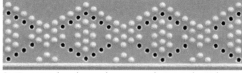

3. Turn to back, emboss on diagonal grid.

Example 3

1. Perforate pattern as shown.

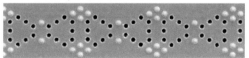

2. Turn to back and emboss.

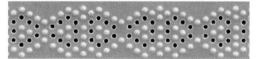

3. Transfer to diagonal grid and emboss.

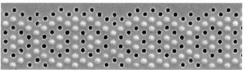

4. Turn to front, perforate on diagonal grid.

Noel

Ingredients

Groovi Grids: *Diagonal Border Pattern Grid No.1* GRO-GG-40354-14,
Diagonal Basic Piercing Grid Border GRO-GG-40383-14.
Groovi A5² Plates: *Nested Squares* GRO-PA-40037-03,
Christmas Banners GRO-LW-40430-03,
Mistletoe & Wreath Accessories GRO-LW-40434-03.
Groovi A4² Plates: *Winter Scene-Cat* GRO-WI-40450-15,
Winter Scene-Children GRO-WI-40448-15 , *Twiggy Wreath* GRO-LW-40433-15.

To Make

1. Emboss the design on regular parchment. You will be using the fifth and sixth nested squares for the double frame, so slot that plate into the Plate Mate, then place the large Winter Scene plate on top, and emboss the tree into place BEFORE embossing the frame. Add all the embellishments and dangles next.

2. Colour in on the back using Perga Colours and/or Distress Markers

3. Emboss and perforate Border pattern 7 outside the square (see example 1, page 57).

4. Cut and mount on dark pink parchment and then black card with brads. Attach to a white card blank.

5. Add some sparkle with a Wink of Stella pen on the front.

Bluebells

DESIGNED USING PATTERN SEVEN

Ingredients

Groovi Grids: *Diagonal Border Pattern Grid No.1* GRO-GG-40354-14,
Diagonal Basic Piercing Grid Border GRO-GG-40383-14.
Groovi A5² Plates: *Nested Squares* GRO-PA-40037-03,
Sprig Swirl GRO-FL-40041-03
Groovi Border Plates: *Floral Squares Fuchsia* GRO-FL-40421-09
Cake Decorations GRO-WE-40377-09

To Make

1. Emboss the design on blue parchment. Start with the boxes and frames, then fill with the designs. Smallest box is fifth line from the inside on the Nested Square. Next box is eighth from the inside, and outer frame is the second box in from the outside.

2. Apply a little gentle whitework to the leaves and flowers. Colour in on the back using Perga Liners.

3. Emboss and perforate Border Pattern 7 inside the middle square and outside the main square (see example 2, page 57).

4. Cut and mount on regular parchment and black card using brads, then attach this to a white card blank.

5. Add some sparkle with a Wink of Stella pen on the front.

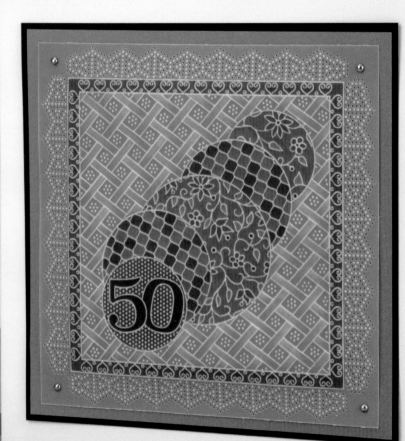

Sweet 50

DESIGNED USING PATTERN SEVEN

Ingredients

Groovi Grids: *Diagonal Border Pattern Grid No.1* GRO-GG-40354-14, *Diagonal Basic Piercing Grid Border* GRO-GG-40383-14.
Groovi Baby Plates: *Small Nested Circle* GRO-PA-40172-01, *Open Number 0* GRO-WO-40452-01, *Open Number 5* GRO-WO-40457-01.
Groovi Border Plates: *Cake Decorations* GRO-WE-40377-09.
Groovi A5² Plates: *Nested Squares* GRO-PA-40037-03, *Woven Trellis* GRO-PA-40131-03, *Large Lace Netting* GRO-PA-40339-03, *Floral Circle* GRO-FL-40446-03.

To Make

1. Emboss your design on pink parchment (third and fourth square in on the Nested Squares for the double-frame). Emboss various sized circles, starting with the one at the front. These can then be filled with elements from the floral and netting plates.

2. Colour in on the back, using Perga Colour pens or Distress markers

3. Emboss 'flowers' between Woven Trellis using Border Pattern 4.

4. Emboss and perforate Border Pattern 7 outside the square (see example 3, page 57).

5. Cut and mount on regular parchment and black card with brads, and attach this to a white card blank.

The **Big** Project

Ingredients

Groovi Grids: *Diagonal Border Pattern Grid No.1* GRO-GG-40354-14, *Diagonal Basic Piercing Grid Border* GRO-GG-40383-14.
Groovi Baby Plates: *Abstract Spruce Tree* GRO-TR-40221-01,
Groovi A5^2 Plates: *Nested Squares* GRO-PA-40037-03,
Nested Hearts GRO-PA-40094-03, *Mountains & Hills* GRO-LA-40007-03.

Lone Spruce

Now that we have studied this clever diagonal pattern plate, let's put our knowledge into practice, and combine all these new patterns in one piece of artwork.

The Lone Spruce is a wonderful example of how something very beautiful is actually very simple - when you know how!

Emboss the design on light blue parchment - all embossing is undertaken on the back.

- Emboss the first and second squares in from the outside.
- Emboss a rectangle using the eighth square from the outside.
- Using the second square from the inside as a guide, emboss a line inside and across the square, avoiding the rectangle area.
- Emboss the tree in the rectangle.
- Emboss a second rectangle around the tree
- Emboss the landscape and sun into place in the background.
- Emboss dangling hearts.

Diagonal Border Pattern Piercing Plate 1

- Emboss the entire Diagonal Pattern Border Grid just as it comes, across the lower panel of the square.
- Emboss lines between each of the border patterns, to separate them.
- Emboss Border Pattern 4 in the double square outline.
- In the double rectangle outline, emboss Border Pattern 2, leaving out the middle dots in the diamonds.

Basic Diagonal Grid

- Emboss dots in the three dangling hearts using the basic diagonal grid.
- Emboss random dots on the tree.

Colour on the back - Distress Markers for a translucent look.

Tree - *Pine Needles, Walnut Stain, Gathered Twigs.*

Sun and double outline frames - *Squeezed Lemonade, Carved Pumpkin.*

Landscape - *Twisted Citron, Mowed Lawn, Peeled Paint.*

Hearts - *Chipped Sapphire.*

Pattern Grid Sampler - *Broken China, Cracked Pistachio.*

magnifier A

magnifier B

Perforate on front.

- Align with work on the front, align the diamonds from Border Pattern 2 on the border pattern plate and perforate the hole in the middle (See magnifier A).
- Align Border Pattern 4 on the Basic Diagonal Grid and perforate three vertical holes between each flower (See magnifier B).
- Cut to size just outside the outermost square. There is a very useful thing called the Groovi grip, which can be attached to the back of your ruler. It prevents the ruler sliding on the parchment as you cut.

Making The Outside Border

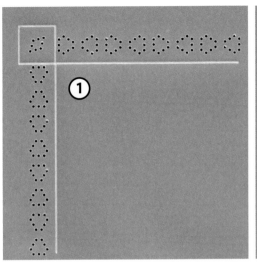

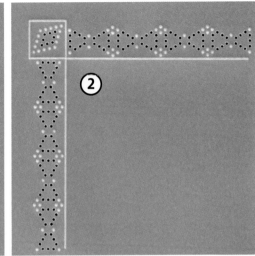

1.

On regular parchment:

- Using the Nested Square plate, emboss the largest square.
- Emboss the smallest square in the corners.
- Perforate the inside diamond on Border Pattern 6 in the corners.
- Perforate the outside large square outlines from Border Pattern 7.

2.

Turn to the back now.

- Emboss the remaining dots on Border Pattern 7.

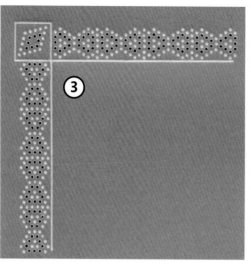

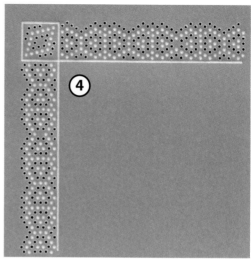

3.

Use the Basic Diagonal Grid.
Emboss another outline of dots surrounding the previously perforated and embossed dots.

4.

Finally, turn to the front again.
Perforate around all the embossed dots on a Basic Diagonal Grid.
Cut the parchment to size just outside the lacework.

Finishing

- Mount the blue parchment artwork onto the regular parchment panel with a lovely lacework, and then black card. Secure using brads.
- Attach your creation onto black card and then onto a white card blank.

It really is quite amazing isn't it? That just a few holes strategically drilled into a plate of acrylic can produce such beautiful lacework is brilliant, isn't it?
So let's see.
Previously, we worked on **Straight Border Pattern Grid No. 1**
This time we got to grips with **Diagonal Border Pattern Grid No. 1**

In Tina's next ii-Book, I think we are ready to ramp it up a notch, and incorporate picot cutting into our gridwork. So we will go back to the **Straight Border Pattern Grid No. 1** and develop a whole new skill set using the same grid.
One snip at a time!

B xx